W0471574

Liebe Schülerin! Lieber Schüler!

Dein viertes Jahr in der NMS oder AHS hast du geschafft und es hat hoffentlich Spaß gemacht!

Damit du mit dem guten Gefühl das nächste Schuljahr beginnen kannst, in Englisch super vorbereitet zu sein, gibt es das Ferienheft „Locker Aufsteigen"!

Du kannst den Stoff der 4. Klasse damit nochmals üben und festigen. Damit es in den Ferien aber nicht allzu „schulisch" zugeht und der Spaß nicht zu kurz kommt, haben wir uns interessante Themen einfallen lassen, die Übungen möglichst abwechslungsreich gestaltet und viele spannende Quizfragen und Rätsel eingebaut.

Die Kapitel sind jeweils in drei Abschnitte eingeteilt: „Do you remember?" ist die Aufwärmphase, im Abschnitt „Practice" vertiefst du die Lerninhalte nochmals und „For Whiz Kids" ist für diejenigen unter euch, die Herausforderungen lieben. Wer dann auch noch den Progress Check am Ende gut meistert, ist ein Profi im Umgang mit dem Lernstoff der 4. Klasse!

Für Momente, in denen du vielleicht doch nochmal gern einen Blick auf die eine oder andere Regel oder einen Merksatz werfen willst, haben wir diese in QR-Codes „verpackt", die du mit deinem Smartphone einscannen kannst (Apps findest du in deinem Apple/Android-Store). Der Link führt dich zum PDF mit den zur jeweiligen Übung gehörigen Regeln aus den „Aufsteigen"-Bänden. Falls du kein Smartphone hast, findest du alle PDFs auch auf unserer Website (www.ggverlag.at) – klicke auf den Button „Unterrichtsmaterial" und suche unter „Locker Aufsteigen" den Band, den du brauchst, sowie die dazugehörige Datei.

Ein Lösungsheft zur Selbstkontrolle liegt natürlich auch bei! Außerdem haben wir jeweils einige Übungen pro Kapitel ausgesucht, bei denen du eintragen kannst, wie viele Punkte du erreicht hast. Wenn du alle diese erreichten Punkte am Ende zusammenzählst, kannst du dein Können bewerten und hinten im Heft nachlesen, wie „fit" du für das nächste Schuljahr bist.

„Locker Aufsteigen in Englisch 4" bereitet dich aber nicht nur bestens aufs nächste Schuljahr vor, es hilft dir auch beim **Erreichen der Bildungsstandards** in den Bereichen Lesen und Schreiben.

Wir wünschen dir viel Spaß bei den Übungen und schöne Ferien!
Vielleicht kannst du ja, wenn du in den Ferien in England, Amerika, Kanada, Australien oder Neuseeland bist, dein Wissen gleich praktisch anwenden!

Astrid Berger und **Gabriele Broniowski**

Session 1 – Ireland

Do you remember?

1 **Can you find 15 words that have something to do with Ireland?**

N	F	H	Q	B	R	V	L	K	M	H	I	C	X	W	A	T	M	O	V	G	R	D	X	R
U	N	U	T	C	O	Y	L	K	I	J	P	O	T	A	T	O	E	S	Y	G	A	R	C	Y
Z	R	K	J	K	J	W	R	H	D	L	H	I	H	X	O	G	S	W	J	W	I	J	O	B
V	Q	C	A	F	C	M	E	P	S	O	K	B	T	S	H	E	E	P	P	I	N	J	L	M
V	E	N	L	S	Z	P	Q	S	U	T	U	E	N	A	J	G	R	D	U	B	L	I	N	J
H	X	V	N	Q	B	R	O	L	Z	P	V	B	N	H	S	H	A	M	R	O	C	K	Z	D
K	R	O	T	T	H	O	B	E	Y	C	J	X	L	N	V	J	E	L	I	H	J	N	R	V
Z	W	R	I	S	Z	T	F	P	H	L	X	R	W	Y	Y	B	I	R	Y	B	Z	W	Y	H
J	R	E	I	W	S	E	C	R	P	B	X	A	N	S	D	W	A	Y	J	H	S	Z	G	C
C	V	R	H	A	U	S	R	E	P	A	B	Y	H	K	S	V	R	R	X	H	F	G	U	F
P	I	O	F	B	P	T	N	C	Z	M	X	B	Z	T	O	E	O	G	Z	C	F	M	I	U
D	M	L	F	Q	P	A	R	H	H	Y	R	N	V	D	J	I	X	Q	X	W	X	B	N	L
W	E	G	I	D	C	N	E	A	B	W	K	G	L	E	N	D	A	L	O	U	G	H	N	G
B	D	C	E	A	X	T	Z	U	U	N	N	E	Q	P	W	W	Q	P	L	Y	D	P	E	P
V	D	T	L	U	K	S	T	N	Y	C	L	I	F	F	S	O	F	M	O	H	E	R	S	O
H	S	T	U	H	J	O	C	A	T	H	O	L	I	C	S	S	V	P	T	M	T	L	S	X
A	Y	N	L	W	B	A	L	A	Q	Q	B	Y	H	V	L	B	A	V	F	M	R	R	X	A

2 **Fill in the correct tense (past simple, past progressive, past perfect):**

14

Last summer Paul and Samantha ______ (want) to fly to Ireland with their parents. They ______ (already/pack) their suitcases and ______ (wait) for the taxi to take them to the airport. When the taxi ______ (arrive) their mother ______ (look) into her handbag to make sure the tickets ______ (be) there. But she ______ (not/can) find them. So everybody ______ (start) looking for the tickets in the whole house while the taxi driver ______ (wait) in front of the house. Suddenly their father ______ (remember) that he ______ (put) the tickets into his suitcase. Quickly he ______ (take) them out and they ______ (get) into the taxi. They ______ (arrive) at the airport just in time to catch their plane.

3

Practice

Look at the picture and write down what the members of her family were doing when Mrs. Brown came home:

1. When Mrs. Brown came home, her eldest daughter Sally
   ______________________________.
2. Tom ______________________.
3. The twins ______________________.
4. Her husband ______________________ on the sofa ______________________ ______________________ TV.
5. The baby ______________________.

4

Fill in the gaps using personal and possessive pronouns:

1. Hello Mike, this is ________ brother Bill. I don't know if you have met ________.
2. Hey girls, what do ________ think? Shall ________ buy tickets for the concert? ________ father could get ________.
3. Peter always talks about ________ cat Susi. I'd really like to see ________.
4. Paula and I are in the same class. Yesterday ________ teacher asked ________ to prepare a presentation together.

5 For Whiz Kids

Read the text about St. Patrick and mark the sentences *true* or *false*:

The story of St. Patrick

St. Patrick, the patron saint of Ireland, lived at the end of the 4th and the beginning of the 5th century. He was born in Wales. When he was fourteen years old he was taken to Ireland as a slave. For six years he had to work very hard on a farm. He often prayed to God and one night God told him that he had to escape. Patrick managed to get to a port where he asked the captain of a ship transporting wolfhounds to France to take him on board. The captain didn't want to have a slave on his ship and sent Patrick away. But when the ship was about to leave the pier the hounds began to bark and to behave like mad. So the ship had to return. When they tried again later the same thing happened. Now Patrick saw his chance. He told the captain that he would calm the dogs if the captain took him to France. The captain agreed and really, when Patrick boarded the ship the hounds became quiet. So Patrick got to France and from there back to his family in Wales.

Soon Patrick found out that he wanted to become a priest. Later he returned to Ireland to become a missionary. It was Easter when he arrived in Ireland. Patrick and the other priests, who had come with him, decided that they wanted to light a fire. That night was also a very special night for the Irish people who were no Christians. They were celebrating the coming of spring. Usually their king lit a fire as a sign for all the other people to light their fires. But now Patrick had lit his fire first. The Irish king was very angry and sent people to put out Patrick's fire but they couldn't. Only Patrick could do it.

Soon Patrick began to talk to the people. They were surprised that he could speak their language so very well. He told them about the Christian God and about Jesus. So he brought Christianity to Ireland.

A legend says that Patrick drove the snakes from Ireland. He was standing on a hill and with a wooden stick drove the snakes into the sea. There are really no snakes in Ireland but this may be because Ireland is an island separated from the continent, so the snakes could not get there. Besides, snakes were a common symbol in many old Irish religions. The story of St. Patrick and the snakes is a symbol of Christianity replacing pagan (heidnisch) religions in Ireland.

Each year on March 17th the Irish all over the world celebrate St. Patrick's Day.

	true	false
1. St. Patrick was born in Ireland.	☐	☐
2. When he was a teenager he lived in Ireland.	☐	☐
3. By ship Patrick travelled to London.	☐	☐
4. He was very afraid of dogs.	☐	☐
5. Later Patrick became a priest and went back to Ireland.	☐	☐
6. At Easter all the Irish Christians lit fires.	☐	☐
7. Patrick couldn't speak the language of the Irish.	☐	☐
8. With a fire Patrick killed all the snakes in Ireland.	☐	☐
9. Today there are no snakes in Ireland.	☐	☐
10. St. Patrick's Day is in March.	☐	☐

Session 2 – Investigating a crime

Do you remember?

1 **Match the English and the German words:**

Zeuge

blackmail

erpressen

murderer

Waffe

weapon

Mörder

crime scene

victim

evidence

investigate

Beweis

Verdächtige/r

verhören

suspect

Tatort

untersuchen

question

Opfer

witness

2 **Unscramble the crime words:**

1. VICENEDE ____________ this helps the police to find the perpetrator (Täter)
2. GRABRUL ____________ somebody who breaks into a house or flat to steal something
3. PANOWE ____________ instrument used to hurt or kill somebody
4. MECIR SENEC ____________ place where a crime happened
5. HEFTI ____________ person who steals things
6. RUDMER ____________ crime in which a person is killed
7. GAINSTEVETI ____________ look into a crime
8. SENTWIS ____________ person who has watched a crime or an accident

Practice

3 **Fill in the correct passive forms:**

1. The old man ______________________ (kill) by the burglar. (past tense)
2. This case ______________________ (investigate) for two months. (present perfect)
3. The murderer ______________________ (not/catch) yet. (present perfect)
4. Last week the criminal ______________________ (arrest) by the police. (past tense)
5. The manager ______________________ (blackmail) by a former employee. (present progressive)
6. The burglar ______________________ (send) to prison for two months. (past tense)

7. After the weapon ______________________ (find) the police looked for fingerprints. (past perfect)
8. The suspect ______________________ (question) by the police. (present progressive)
9. The thief ______________________ (sentence) to 5 months in prison. (past tense)

4

Fill in the past perfect tense:

1. After the police ______________________ (catch) the suspect, they started questioning him.
2. As soon as they ______________________ (identify) the victim, they contacted the victim's relatives.
3. After he ______________________ (shoot) his wife, he called the police.
4. He ______________________ (just/hack) into the bank's computer when the Internet went down. Tough luck!
5. The old lady ______________________ (just/withdraw – abheben) some money from the cash machine when a mugger hit her on the head and stole the money.
6. After they ______________________ (find) the dead body, they phoned the police.

5

7

Complete the following if-clauses:

1. If you don't lock your bike, somebody ______________________ (steal) it.
2. If they ______________________ (have) more money, they would buy a burglar alarm.
3. What ______________________ (you/do) if somebody attacked you?
4. If I witnessed a crime, I ______________________ (call) the police.
5. If they had a suspect, they ______________________ (question) him/her.
6. If the fingerprints are on record, they ______________________ (can/arrest) the thief.
7. What will you do if somebody ______________________ (break) into your house?

6

7

Fill in past or past perfect tense:

1. She ______________________ (be) on her way to the train station. Suddenly she decided to go back because she wasn't quite sure, if she ______________________ (lock) the front door.
2. The witness ______________________ (give) them a good description of the robbers.
3. He could not remember where he ______________________ (park) his car.
4. Police cars were standing in front of the bank because some masked men ______________________ (try) to rob the bank.
5. " ______________________ (you/watch) CSI New York last Monday?" – "No, I couldn't because I ______________________ (must) study for a test."

For Whiz Kids

7

Change the sentences from active to passive:

1. Three men robbed the bank.

   ____

2. The police will question the suspect.

   ____

3. A tall man attacked Fiona and took her handbag.

   ____

4. An unknown person is blackmailing Mr. Winters.

   ____

5. A famous director will shoot a crime thriller in our village.

   ____

6. A witness reports a crime.

   ____

8

Find the famous detective:

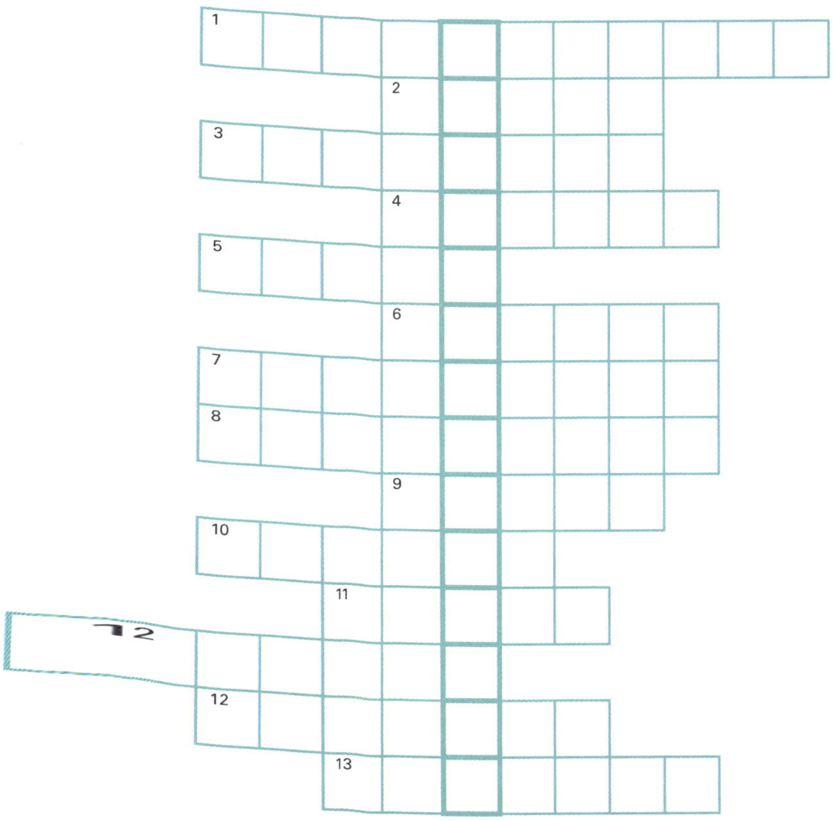

1. this is what the police do to solve a crime: i _ _ _ _ _ _ _ _ _ _
2. this is what you do when you fire a gun: s _ _ _ _
3. another word for "proof": e _ _ _ _ _ _ _
4. this is what the police do when they catch a criminal: a _ _ _ _ _
5. you do this when you take something that belongs to another person: s _ _ _ _
6. wooden box that dead people are buried in: c _ _ _ _ _
7. person who tries to solve a crime: d _ _ _ _ _ _ _ _
8. this is the English word for "erpressen": b _ _ _ _ _ _ _ _
9. a person who steals something is called a: t _ _ _ _
10. a gun is a: w _ _ _ _ _
11. the police try to s _ _ _ _ a case
12. the person who is attacked, robbed or murdered is called a: v _ _ _ _ _
13. a person who sees a crime happening is called a: w _ _ _ _ _ _
14. a person who maybe has committed a crime is a: s _ _ _ _ _ _

Session 3 – Getting around in a big city

Do you remember?

1 **Unscramble the letters and write down the things you may find in a big city:**

inrat natisto	
regnodurnud	
athrete	
acnemi	
ritopra	

2 **Where are they?**

1. Bill is in ______________________________.
2. Sally ______________________________.
3. Ben and Mary ______________________________.
4. Susan ______________________________.
5. Paul ______________________________.

Practice

3 **Underline the correct word in these sentences:**

5

1. You should always wear a crash helmet when you *ride/drive* a bike.
2. Pete *drives/goes* to school by bus.
3. Trains to the airport *travel/run* every hour.
4. Yesterday I *missed/lost* the school bus.
5. He was late because of the traffic *queue/jam.*

4 **Tell your friend what Mr. Anderson said about life in a big city:**

Mr. Anderson: I have been living in a big city for many years. First I enjoyed the busy life there. Now I still like it but I have other plans for the future. Next year I'm going to move to a small village in the country. I'll let you know what life is like there.

Mr. Anderson said that ...

He told us that ...

Then he explained that ...

He added that ...

He promised that ...

5 **Change each sentence to direct speech:**

1. She said that Peter often went skiing in winter.

   ____.

2. Ann said that they had left on Monday.

   ____.

3. The teacher said that he would talk to my parents.

   ____.

4. Tina said that she was working.

   ____.

5. Tom said that he had just talked to Sam.

   ____.

6 **Complete the sentences using *say* or *tell*:**

1. Ann __________ goodbye to me and left.
2. Simon, __________ us about your holiday. Did you have a nice time?
3. Don't just stand there! __________ something!
4. I wonder where Sue is. She __________ she would be here at 8 o'clock.
5. Jack __________ me that he was fed up with his job.
6. The doctor __________ that I should rest for at least a week.
7. Don't __________ anybody what I __________. It's a secret just between us.

7 **Put the sentences into indirect speech:**

1. "You must lock the door when you leave the flat", Sally said.

   ____.

2. Simon said, "I had to wait 20 minutes for the train."

   ____.

3. Mary said, "We will buy tickets for the concert in the afternoon."

   ____.

4. Peter shouted, "I have not broken your glasses!"

   ____.

8 **Where are the things?**

1. The keys are ______________________________
2. The English book is ______________________________.
3. The mobile phone is ______________________________.
4. The red jacket is ______________________________.
5. The tea cup is ______________________________.
6. The concert tickets are ______________________________.

9 **Underline the correct word:**

6

1. He always goes for a walk *in/at* the evening.
2. I'm not going *at/to* school today.
3. Did you see the new show *in/on* TV yesterday?
4. The teacher walked *into/in* the classroom and sat down.
5. You have to wait *before/in front of* the theatre.
6. The Browns want to buy a house *at/in* the country.

For Whiz Kids

10 **Fill in the correct prepositions:**

__________ the morning many people use the underground to go to work. Most of them travel __________ 7 and 10 o'clock. Then there is always a queue __________ the ticket machines. The trains are very crowded, too.

__________ 10 o'clock the situation gets better. Fewer people use the underground then.

Lots of people also go to work __________ car. Some of them live __________ places that have no good public transport, others don't want to fight __________ a seat on crowded trains.

I live __________ an underground station, which is very practical and saves time in the morning.

Session 4 – Learning about jobs

Do you remember?

1 **What are their jobs?**

1. Sandra explains mathematics to children. She is a _____.
2. Mr. Smith helps people who have toothache. He is a _____.
3. Tim makes bread and rolls. He is a _____.
4. Paul repairs cars. He is a _____.
5. Alice sells clothes to people in a big store. She is a _____.
6. Mrs. Anderson works in a restaurant where she serves the food. She is a _____.
7. Andrew catches criminals. He is a _____.

2 **Complete the definitions:**

1. A vet _____.
2. A surgeon _____.
3. An architect _____.
4. A secretary _____.
5. An engineer _____.

Practice

3 **Complete the sentences using the correct form of a word from the box:**

lawyer gardener soldier fire fighter nurse architect scientist

1. The man, who had been arrested, wanted to talk to his _____.
2. Many _____ were killed during the war.
3. The _____ changed Mr. Brown's bandage.
4. Once a year the _____ cuts the trees.
5. Sheldon is a _____ and works at the university.
6. After 9/11 the _____ were celebrated as heroes.
7. The Guggenheim Museum was designed by a famous _____.

4 **Choose the best word for each space (see page 12):**

My brother has got a new (1) _____ in the best restaurant in town. He does not work in the kitchen because he is no (2) _____, he is a (3) _____. He takes people's (4) _____ and brings them their food and drinks.
Two months ago he saw a/an (5) _____ in the newspaper which said that they were looking for someone with a lot of (6) _____.

He wrote an e-mail to the manager and was asked to come for a/an (7) ______________.
The manager liked him and he was (8) ______________________ the job.

1. **A.** employment	**B.** work	**C.** job
2. **A.** cook	**B.** cooker	**C.** cooks
3. **A.** waiter	**B.** waitress	**C.** waiting
4. **A.** wish	**B.** orders	**C.** wishes
5. **A.** note	**B.** commercial	**C.** advertisement
6. **A.** experts	**B.** experience	**C.** history
7. **A.** talk	**B.** review	**C.** interview
8. **A.** offered	**B.** gave	**C.** told

5

At the job interview Paul was asked a lot of questions. Put them into reported speech:

5

1. "Where did you see our advertisement?"
   The manager asked Paul ____.
2. "Have you worked at a restaurant before?"
   He wanted to know ____.
3. "Why do you want this job?"
   The manager asked him ____.
4. "Can you work in a team?"
   He wanted to know ____.
5. "When will you be able to start?"
   He asked Paul ____.

6

What did the people want to know? Complete the sentences using reported speech:

e. g. Bruno wanted to know ...

7 **Fill in the missing words to make correct comparisons:**

1. It takes ______ (long) to become a doctor ______ to become a shop assistant.
2. I think that was the ______ (bad) job interview I ever had.
3. Working in an office is not ______ (interesting) working in a laboratory.
4. I did not get paid ______ (much) in my old job ______ in my new one.
5. Cars are ______ (expensive) bicycles.
6. Being a fire fighter is ______ (dangerous) being a teacher.
7. Last night's show was ______ (funny) today's.

For Whiz Kids

8 **Read the most common reasons why people are not successful in a job interview. Then write an e-mail to your friend, who is going to have a job interview, telling him/her how he/she should behave.**

Not dressed properly
Too aggressive
Unable to express themselves clearly
Not enthusiastic enough
Don't really know what they want. Have no plans.
Too nervous
Only interested in money
Not willing to start at the bottom
Not polite
Speak ill about former employer
Cannot make eye contact
Late for the interview
Ask no questions about the company
Cannot give direct answers when questioned

Session 5 – Eating the right kind of food

Do you remember?

1 **Match the adjectives about food with the definitions:**

1. harmful
2. healthy
3. nutritious
4. tasty
5. filling
6. artificial

- a man-made, not natural
- b providing the things your body needs
- c having a pleasant flavour
- d bad for your body or health
- e has good effects on your body
- f makes you feel full

2 **Do you know these food words:**

Practice

3 **Complete the if-sentences (type 3):**

6

1. You would not have got sick, if you ________ (not/eat) so much ice cream.
2. If I had known that you are a vegetarian, I ________ (not/offer) you any meat.
3. If she had bought carrots, she ________ (can/make) a tasty carrot soup.
4. If he ________ (use) more spices, the dish would have tasted better.
5. They would not have had to go to a fast food restaurant, if you ________ (cook) dinner.
6. I ________ (not/order) the soup if I had known that it contained mushrooms.

4 **Fast food versus junk food. Read the text, then answer the questions:**

Junk food contains high levels of calories, salt, sugar and fat, which can cause health problems. Fries, chips, cookies and sweets all fall under the junk food category. Fast food, on the other hand, can be healthy. Think of salads, an apple, a banana, or a glass of milk.
If you are the kind of person who always gets up too late in the morning, and who just barely catches the bus to school, then you surely know what fast food is. There's just time enough to slap some cheese or meat or leaves between two slices of bread as breakfast as you rush out of the house.
Fast food has been around for ages, though, and it is not necessarily harmful. It's food that can be made in a short time. So sandwiches, salads, eggs and milk are all fast food.
Junk food, however, is a totally different matter. If you regularly order extra cheese with your pizza, big fries with your burger, or if you love those sugary soft drinks then you're in for clogged arteries and a bulging waist. It's true fries taste good and the soft drink gives a kick. But do you really want to take up two seats in the airplane or block the aisle in the supermarket? Junk food is low on important nutrients and high on fat, sodium and calories. If you eat a lot of junk food, you put on weight and develop health problems.

1. What is wrong with junk food?

   ____

2. What examples of healthy fast food does the text mention?

   ____

3. Why is junk food bad for our health?

   ____

4. What is the definition of fast food?

   ____

5 **Complete the if-sentences (all types):**

1. If you follow the recipe, the dish ____________ (be) okay.
2. If I met Jamie Oliver, I ____________ (ask) him for an autograph.
3. Don't eat meat, if you ____________ (feel) sorry for the animals.
4. If you don't want to put on weight, ____________ (not/eat) a lot of junk food!
5. If he had not been in a hurry, he ____________ (eat) a proper breakfast.
6. If you listened to your doctor, you ____________ (know) that too much junk food can clog your arteries.

6 **Use the past or past perfect tense:**

1. After he ____________ (finish) the pizza, he felt a bit sick.

2. She ______________ (decide) to become a vegetarian after she had watched a film about how animals were killed.
3. When the waiter ______________ (come) to their table, they ______________ (ask) for the menu.
4. He asked his mum to prepare his favourite dish, because he ______________ (not/eat) it in a long time.
5. When she went out for lunch, she ______________ (order) a salad.

For Whiz Kids

7

Read the text, then do the true/false exercise:

5

People who do not eat meat or fish are called vegetarians. Vegetarians eat food like vegetables, fruits, beans and grains. Some vegetarians eat or drink animal products, like eggs and milk.

There are many reasons for not eating meat. Some think that it is wrong to kill animals; others think that eating meat is bad for our health and the world in general. Some people say land used for animals can be used to grow food. Some people may become vegetarians because their religion tells them not to eat animals.

Vegetarians who do not eat milk, eggs or any other dairy products are called vegans. Vegans will not use animal products like leather, either, but many vegetarians do use animal products. Some people who call themselves vegetarians and eat fish or sea food are not really vegetarians, because fish and sea creatures are also animals. There are also many people who are not vegetarians, but do not eat a lot of red or white meat.

	true	false
1. People who do not eat any red meat are called vegetarians.	☐	☐
2. Some people become vegetarians because they do not like the taste of meat.	☐	☐
3. Some people do not eat meat because of their religion.	☐	☐
4. Vegans are vegetarians who do not eat any dairy products, either.	☐	☐
5. Vegetarians do not use any animal products.	☐	☐

8

–Ing form or infinitive?

1. Martin has bought a book on Organic Farming. He wants ______________ (know) more about it.
2. She has tried ______________ (give) up meat, but she says it is very difficult for her.
3. He insisted on ______________ (buy) Fairtrade products.
4. My dad dreams of ______________ (change) his job. He'd like to be a chef.
5. She is a vegetarian. She does not miss ______________ (eat) meat.

Session 6 – Going to Australia

Do you remember?

1 **The Australia Quiz – do you know the correct answers?**

1. The capital of Australia is
   a) Sydney
   b) Darwin
   c) Canberra

2. The native inhabitants of Australia are called
   a) Maori
   b) Indians
   c) Aborigines

3. Australia is
   a) 85 times
   b) 91 times
   c) 63 times bigger than Austria.

4. When it is 10 am in Vienna it is
   a) 6 pm in Canberra
   b) 7 am in Canberra
   c) 4 pm in Canberra

5. The Kakadu National Park is
   a) three hours from Sydney
   b) two hours from Darwin
   c) one hour from Perth

6. Which animal does not belong to Australia?
   a) Panda bear
   b) Koala bear
   c) Kangaroo

2 **Do you know what is described here?**

1. It is the largest coral reef in the world. ______________________
2. It is a smaller version of a kangaroo. ______________________
3. It is a building in Sydney that looks like a huge sailing boat. ______________________
4. It is an instrument played by the Aborigines. ______________________
5. It is a huge red rock right in the middle of Australia. ______________________
6. This is what Australians call the remote bush country of Australia. ______________________

Practice

3

Complete the if-sentences:

1. If you ______ (want) to spend some time in the Australian outback, make sure you take enough water with you.
2. If I had gone to Australia last year, I ______ (visit) the Great Barrier Reef.
3. If they went to Sydney, they ______ (can/take) a picture of the famous Opera House.
4. If the weather is nice, Jeff and Jenny ______ (climb) to the top of The Harbour Bridge in Sydney.
5. If you are ill but live far away from a town, the flying doctors ______ (help) you.
6. If you ______ (be) an Aborigine, Uluru would not just be a tourist attraction.
7. If they ______ (go) to Darwin, they could have visited Kakadu National Park.

4

19

Fill in the correct tenses:

In August Mona and her family ______ (fly) to Australia.
It ______ (take) them almost two days to get to Sydney, the first stop of their trip. They ______ (stay) at a nice hotel and ______ (do) a lot of sightseeing. On their first day they ______ (go) to The Harbour Bridge because from the top you ______ (have) a wonderful view. Mona's mum ______ (not climb) to the top because she ______ (be) afraid of heights. They also ______ (take) photos of Sydney's famous Opera House and the beautiful harbour.
From Sydney they ______ (fly) to Alice Springs because they ______ (want) to drive to Ayers Rock from there.
At Ayers Rock Mona met a tourist who said," If I ______ (know) how dangerous it is to climb Uluru, I ______ (not/ try) it. I almost ______ (break) my leg."
From Alice spring Mona's family ______ (fly) to Darwin because they ______ (want) to explore Kakadu National Park. Mona's brother Simon ______ (love) the goannas and the cave paintings best.
On the flight back to Austria Mona's dad said, "Next time we ______ (go) to the Great Barrier Reef because it ______ (be) the largest coral reef in the world."

Use reported speech:

1. Mona's friend Alice asked, "What did you like best about Australia?"

2. Mona's dad said, "We must rent a car if we want to go to Ayers Rock."

3. Simon wanted to know, "When did the Aborigines arrive in Australia?"

4. Simon wanted to know, "How far away is Sydney from Perth?"

5. Mona asked the guide, "What do Koala bears eat?"

For Whiz Kids

Do the crossword:

Across:
1. He discovered Australia in 1770
2. They were the first white settlers in Australia
3. The Great Barrier Reef is made up of these

Down:
1. That's what the native people are called
2. It is the name of the remote bush country
3. a ridge of rock, sand, or coral, the top of which lies close to the surface of the sea

Session 7 – Talking about (unusual) hobbies

Do you remember?

1 **Fill in the chart:**

She collects soft toys.

We will take part in an extreme ironing competition.

He is reorganizing his stamp collection.

They dressed up as historical figures.

He has copied about 50 paintings by famous artists.

She was building a fantastic sand castle.

They had given away their tea bag collection.

He has been carving wooden animals since he was seven.

TENSE	SENTENCE
Present tense simple	
Present tense progressive/continuous	
Past tense simple	
Past tense progressive/continuous	
Present perfect simple	
Present perfect progressive/continuous	
Past perfect simple	
Future tense	

2 **Can you find the hobbies?**

CORK BLIMGNIC		GENCINF	
SHORE GIRNID		DANRIGE	
LISANIG		TINTKNIG	

Practice

3 **Read the three texts about unusual hobbies, then do the tasks:**

Collecting tea bag covers/envelopes

Gerda is 29 years old and lives in Switzerland. She has been collecting teabags for seven years and at the moment she has about 12,000 teabags. Well, she actually collects the wrappers or envelopes, not the part you use to brew tea. Some people think it's strange to collect teabags, but in fact there are a lot of people who

do the same. In Belgium and The Netherlands there are more than 200 people who share this hobby. Gerda exchanges teabags with people from all over the world, even The United States of America.

Extreme ironing

Extreme ironing is a competitive sport, also known as EI. Extreme ironing consists of ironing clothing in different, usually extreme, situations like while rock climbing, surfing, or scuba diving. Extreme ironing can be and pretty much has been performed everywhere. Extreme ironing was invented back in 1997 in Leicester, Midlands, England by a man named Phil Shaw. In 2003, the documentary *Extreme Ironing: Pressing for Victory* was aired on Britain's Channel 4. Because of this documentary, the sport finally began to gain real international attention. The world of EI is quite fascinating, and the participants come from all over the world.

Working with duct tape (Klebeband)

Anna's hobby is duct tape art. Her creations include shoes, clothes, jewelry, cards and sculptures – even a model of Shakespeare's Globe Theatre (which she used as a home for her turtle).
Most people aren't quite sure what to make of Anna's fascination with duct tape. "They laugh and make fun of me," she says, "but they always come to me when they need an adhesive."
Laughter isn't the only problem Anna has to deal with while pursuing her hobby. "Duct tape is very sticky," she says. When she was making her skirt, the duct tape kept sticking to places it wasn't supposed to. She admits that wearing duct tape is slightly uncomfortable because it's stiff and doesn't breathe very well.

a. Answer the following questions:

1. For how long has Gerda been collecting tea bags?

____

2. When and by whom was extreme ironing invented?

____

3. What does Anna create with duct tape?

____

4. Why are duct tape clothes not very comfortable?

____

b. Tick *true* or *false*:

	true	false
1. There are only a handful of people who collect tea bags.	☐	☐
2. Extreme ironing became better known after a BBC documentary in 2003.	☐	☐
3. Extreme ironing can only be performed under water.	☐	☐
4. Anna used duct tape to make a model of Shakespeare's Globe.	☐	☐
5. People make fun of Anna and her hobby.	☐	☐

4

10

Use the past or present perfect tense to complete the dialogues:

1. **A** When I was a child I ______________ (collect) buttons. I ______________ (love) the different colours, shapes and sizes. ______________ (you/ever/collect) anything?
   B No, I haven't. I ______________ (never/feel) the need to collect anything.
2. **A** ______________ (you/see) the extreme ironing competitions on TV last night?
   B No, I didn't. I ______________ (must) write an essay for my English class.
3. **A** Two days ago I ______________ (watch) a documentary about unusual hobbies. They ______________ (interview) a person who collects airsick bags.
   B What a crazy idea!
4. **A** ______________ (you/hear) about this exhibition on sand art?
   B Yes, I ______________ (already/see) some posters. I think it is an unusual hobby.

5

Match the questions and answers:

1. Do you have any hobbies?
2. Do you know what taphophilia is?
3. Do you collect stamps?
4. Have you ever heard of sand sculpting?
5. Why are these books special?
6. What is in this box?

a No, I think that is a boring hobby.
b Yes, there was an exhibition on the beach last week.
c They are all signed copies.
d Yes, I love skiing and I collect funny flash drives.
e It is my coin collection.
f It means an unusually strong interest in graves and cemeteries.

For Whiz Kid

6

Read the short texts and ask questions:

She took up horse riding when she was 7 years old.
She loved horses and went riding three to four times a week.
Now she is 14 and still loves riding. But as she has to study a lot for school she can only go horse riding at the weekend.

1. When ______________________________?
2. How often ______________________________?
3. Why ______________________________?

Simon started playing football at the age of six.
He joined a football club when he was 10.
He is quite good at football and he would like to become a professional football player once he has finished school.

4. When ______________________________?
5. At what age ______________________________?
6. What ______________________________?

Session 8 – Finding out about Fairtrade

Do you remember?

1 **Do the crossword puzzle!**

Across
4. Gewinn
7. Waren ausführen
11. Pflanzenschutzmittel
12. Bohnen

Down
1. Entwicklung
2. Gerechtigkeit
3. Bauer
5. Tee
6. Kaffee
8. Projekt
9. Handel
10. Preis

Practice

2 **Read the text about Fairtrade and answer the questions:**

If trade did not exist we could only eat what we grow ourselves and wear what we make ourselves. Nearly everything we eat, wear or use in every day life is a product of trade. Many things we buy are produced in far away countries. Often these countries are poorer or developing countries. The global rules, however, that govern how trade works are made by the rich countries and by big multinational companies.

There are millions of farmers all over the world who work very hard to grow the things we – the people in the rich countries – eat or use every day. Often these farmers don't get a good price for their crop (Ernte). The prices also change very often and very quickly.

This makes it difficult for the farmers to pay for the every-day needs of their families, like food, medicine or school books for their children.

Very often these farmers live in the country, far away from towns and cities. Farming is the only way they can earn a living. They cannot just change their job, because there are no other jobs where they live. So, if they don't get a good price for what they grow, they live in poverty.

Fairtrade tries to pay these farmers a fair price for their crop that makes it possible for them to pay for the things they need. Fairtrade also guarantees the farmers that they will not only buy their crops this year but also the next. That makes it easier for the farmers to know how much money they will have to buy the things they need.

Fairtrade products carry the Fairtrade Mark so that customers here in Europe know that they are buying a product that helps farmers in poorer countries to survive. Lots of Fairtrade products are things that cannot be grown in our country, like cocoa beans for chocolate and cocoa, bananas, tea or coffee.

1. Where do Fairtrade products usually come from?

   ____

2. Who makes the rules of international trade?

   ____

3. Why is it difficult for the farmers to plan what they will be able to buy?

   ____

4. Why don't they just find another job?

   ____

5. How can you recognize Fairtrade products?

   ____

3

7

Put into reported speech:

1. You asked him, "Will you do this for me?"

   ____

2. They asked, "Were you in London last week?"

   ____

3. He said, "I will have finished this paper by five o'clock."

   ____

4. She said, "I am not hungry now."

   ____

5. He told me, "Be quiet!"

   ____

6. She asked me, "Where have you been?"

   ____

7. Tom said to me, "Don't leave the room!"

   ____

4

Complete the sentences with the passive forms of the verbs:

1. Cocoa ____________________ (import) into Austria.
2. In the future farmers in poorer countries ____________________ (pay) a fair price for their crops.
3. Yesterday we ____________________ (take) to the airport by our parents.
4. Fairtrade bananas ____________________ (sell) in many Austrian supermarkets.
5. I ____________________ (never/invite) to the queen's garden party.

5

Make passive sentences:

1. My bag/find/a little girl/ yesterday.

____

2. The baby/baptize(=taufen)/next month.

____

3. I/never before ask/give opening speech.

____

4. Marmalade/make/from oranges.

____

For Whiz Kids

6

Put into reported speech:

A: Oh Inspector, something terrible has happened. I've lost my sweet little dog. He jumped out of my car in front of my house and now I can't find him.
B: Oh dear! First I've got two questions. Where do you live and when did your dog jump out of the car?
A: I live in 10 Pembroke Road, and it was 5 in the afternoon when he jumped out. Please find Timmy, or I will be very unhappy.
B: You must not worry. We will try everything to find him again. And I'm sure he'll come home as soon as he's hungry.
A: Last week he ran away and came home 3 days later. I was really worried.
B: Has any of your neighbours seen your dog since yesterday?
A: I don't know. I'll go home and ask them.
B: Can you please call me, if you find out anything?
A: I certainly will.

Session 9 – Reading good books

Do you remember?

1 **Find the following words in the grid. Then write down their German meaning.**

N	X	V	H	S	I	L	B	U	P
A	S	N	O	V	E	L	R	K	L
R	U	A	N	C	W	D	Q	H	T
R	M	S	C	G	E	T	M	E	Y
A	M	F	O	V	I	O	E	R	S
T	A	J	M	B	V	L	O	O	A
O	R	H	I	P	E	P	P	B	T
R	Y	Z	C	L	R	K	J	U	N
F	W	I	B	R	U	L	B	M	A
D	R	E	T	P	A	H	C	X	F

narrator		review	
novel		summary	
chapter		blurb	
comic		publish	
fantasy		plot	
hero		poem	

2 **Fill in the correct linking words: but, when, because, and, so**

1. Anna loved adventure books __________ she hated horror stories.
2. Bob read "The Hunger Games" __________ watched the movie.
3. Sometimes Molly starts crying __________ she reads a sad story.
4. Susan was too old for children's books, __________ she bought a young adult novel.
5. Adam does not have a lot of books __________ he hates reading.

Practice

3 **Fill in the correct reflexive pronouns:**

7

1. There was nobody to talk to, so the boy started talking to __________.

2. The lady said, "Harry, make ____________ at home. I'll be right back."
3. When the giant looked at ____________ in the mirror for the first time, he was shocked.
4. Last week my mum had to work all day, so my brother and I had to look after ____________.
5. "This is a nice sweater. Did you knit it ____________?" – "Yes, I made it ____________. My grandma showed me how to do it."
6. They did not know where they were and they asked ____________ if they would ever find out of that jungle again.

4

Use linking words (and, but, although, because, or, so, when, who, which…) to connect the sentences:

1. This looks like a good book. Unfortunately it is a bit thick.

   ____

2. Can you recommend a good book? I need to write a book report.

   ____

3. I didn't like "Nightmare". Usually I like horror books.

   ____

4. Jenny has a terrible secret. She is the main character of the book.

   ____

5. Melanie wanted to read a good English book. She asked her teacher for advice.

   ____

6. I have to write a summary of the first chapter. I also have to describe the main character.

   ____

5

Use the word given in capitals at the end of each line to form a word that fits in the gap in the same line:

I was walking down the street when a young man suddenly	
appeared in front of me. "Please, help me!" he said. I could see from	
his ______________ that he was really scared.	**EXPRESS**
He ______________ English with a Polish accent. He gave me a	**SPEAK**
flash drive and said, "There is top secret ______________	**INFORM**
on this memory stick." Then he put a piece of paper with a name	
and an address into my hand. "Contact this person, but do it	
______________ . If anybody finds out you have this	**SECRET**
flash drive, your life will be in danger." I didn't really understand	
what was going on but when I looked up, the young man was	
gone.	

6 **Finish the sentences. Imagine they are from an adventure story. Make them as interesting as possible!**

Suddenly ______________________________

A short time later ______________________________

At that moment ______________________________

After a few minutes ______________________________

Later on ______________________________

Soon ______________________________

Just then ______________________________

7 **What are the American expressions for the following words?**

flat		crisps	
ground floor		underground	
post		chips	
pavement		film	
lift		holidays	

For Whiz Kids

8 **Read the blurb, then write a short text, explaining why you would/would not want to read this book (80-100 words).**

Allie Sheridan's world is falling apart. Her brother's run away from home. Her parents ignore her. And she's just been arrested. Again. This time her parents have had enough. They cut her off from her friends and send her away to boarding school, far from her London friends.
But at Cimmeria Academy, Allie is soon caught up in the strange activities of a secret group of elite students.
When she's attacked late one night the incident sets off a chain of increasingly violent events. As the school begins to seem like a very dangerous place, she finds out that nothing at Cimmeria is what it seems to be. And that she is not who she thought she was.

Session 10 – Exploring space

Do you remember?

1 **Can you find the 12 "space" words in the grid?**

S	P	A	C	E	S	H	U	T	T	L	E
X	I	D	S	X	E	P	F	L	E	K	T
R	W	V	Y	P	Z	N	O	F	N	D	E
O	N	E	I	L	A	L	J	I	A	G	K
B	V	N	S	O	R	B	I	T	L	S	C
O	C	H	T	R	A	E	M	R	P	E	O
T	K	A	G	E	H	Z	Y	G	H	J	R
S	L	X	Z	E	S	R	E	V	I	N	U
A	S	T	R	O	N	A	U	T	D	R	K
Y	M	F	P	I	H	S	E	C	A	P	S

2 **Make predictions about the future:**

In the future there won't be so much/many ______

One of the biggest problems will be ______

There will be ______

People will ______

People won't have to ______ because ______

Practice

3 **Complete the sentences with the –ing form of the verbs from the box:**

see – meet – travel – laugh – apply – read – watch

I enjoy ______ documentaries about space travel.

Ken is interested in ______ about aliens and life in outer space.

My sister is thinking about ______ for a job with NASA.

He is looking forward to ______ a real astronaut for the first time.

I 'm sure that ______ into space will be possible in the future.

My dad remembers ______ the space shuttle disaster of 2003 on TV.

Stop ______ and finish the text about Neil Armstrong, the first man on the Moon.

4

If the verb in bold (fettgedruckt) is correct, put a tick into the box.
If it is wrong, write down the correct form of the verb.

1. I hope I'll be able **to travel** into space when I am older. __________
2. My mum suggested **to watch** a science fiction movie but I hate science fiction. __________
3. I'd really like **visiting** the Kennedy Space Center one day. I have heard so much about it. __________
4. Stop **talking** and start reading the text about astronauts. __________
5. Where is my fantasy book? I remember **putting** it on my desk. __________
6. I can't imagine **to have** to live without a computer or a TV set. __________
7. The children enjoyed **reading** about aliens and robots. __________
8. On the way to the Science Museum we stopped **having** lunch at a fast food restaurant. __________

5

7

Fill in the correct prepositions:

1. Neil Armstrong was the first man to set foot __________ the Moon.
2. The Moon landing was watched __________ half a million people.
3. There are a number of people who would like to travel __________ space.
4. A number of books have been written __________ the Apollo missions.
5. The *Columbia* broke __________ when it re-entered the earth's atmosphere.
6. __________ 1986 the *Challenger* exploded shortly after take-off.
7. The taste __________ food often changes in space.

6

Read the two short texts, then do the true/false exercise:

Men in Black is a movie about two special agents, Kay and Jay. They are members of a top-secret organization whose job it is to monitor and police alien activity on Earth. The two Men in Black have to find an intergalactic terrorist who has arrived on Earth to assassinate two ambassadors from opposing galaxies. The MiB must track down the terrorist and prevent the destruction of Earth.

Independence Day: On July 2nd, communication systems around the world are sent into chaos by a strange atmospheric interference. The military soon find out that a number of enormous objects are on a collision course with Earth. First everyone believes these objects to be meteors, but it turns out that they are gigantic spacecrafts, piloted by a mysterious alien species. Attempts to communicate with the aliens are unsuccessful. David Levinson, an ex-scientist, discovers that the aliens are going to attack major points around the globe in less than a day. On July 3rd, the aliens destroy most of New York, Los Angeles, and Washington. The survivors set out in convoys towards Area 51, a strange government testing ground.

	true	false
1. Agents Kay and Jay are members of a top-secret organisation.	■	■
2. Jay and Kay try to kill two ambassadors from other galaxies.	■	■
3. The huge objects heading towards Earth are meteors.	■	■
4. It is impossible to get into contact with the aliens.	■	■
5. The alien spacecrafts attack big cities around the world.	■	■
6. Nobody survives the attacks.	■	■

For Whiz Kids

7

Find the mistakes (there is one in each sentence) and write down the correct sentences:

1. In the movie MiB agents Kay and Jay were attack by violent aliens.

2. The aliens in Independence Day wanted taking over the world.

3. The Science Museum is close on Christmas Day.

4. The kids are look forward to visiting the Space Center.

5. All of a sudden one of the engines stopped to work but the astronauts did not panic.

8

Write a short story called "The Day the Aliens landed" (180-200 words)

These questions may help you with your story:

- When and where did they land?
- How did they travel from their planet to the planet Earth?
- Why did they come to the planet Earth?
- What kind of aliens were they (friendly, hostile = feindlich)?
- What did they look like?
- What happened after they had landed?

Session 11 – Looking at body art

Do you remember?

1 **Can you remember the parts of the body?**

striw	
enek	
woble	
nifreg	
hutom	
deha	
spil	
notueg	
druhelos	
hostamc	

Practice

2 **Complete the sentences using the correct form of a word from the box:**

6

could	may	can	might	should	must not

1. ________ I take a look at your new tattoo?
2. Sorry, but you ________ smoke in here.
3. You ________ think again before having your lip pierced.
4. ________ you pass the salt, please?
5. Excuse me, ________ I ask you something?
6. I'm not sure where John is. He ________ be in the cellar.

3 **Rewrite the sentences using *might, must* or *can't*:**

1. I'm sure this dragon tattoo is new.

   ____

2. Perhaps I'll have my nose pierced.

   ____

3. I'm sure that is not the right way.

   ____

4. Perhaps you will be sorry if you shave your head.

____

5. I'm sure this is her brother.

____

4 **Complete the sentences using one word for each space:**

1. Peter was not at the party yesterday. He _______ to work.
2. Someone _______ be at home. The lights are on.
3. You _______ really work harder, then your marks will be better.
4. I can't find my keys. Well, I _______ have left them in the car.
5. Do you really _______ to leave now?
6. The baby has been crying for an hour. She _______ be tired soon.
7. You _______ be serious! I'd never do that.
8. _______ I leave the table now?

5 **Complete the if-sentences:**

1. If you really want a pierced nose _______.
2. I would have dyed my hair purple if _______.
3. If we hadn't been late, _______.
4. If the boys were at home, _______.
5. If you really get a tattoo, _______.
6. If getting pierced did not hurt, _______.
7. If I had known how painful getting a tattoo is, _______.

6 **Choose the most suitable word or phrase:**

1. If you start now, you _______ be late for the meeting.
   A. aren't **B.** won't **C.** shall not
2. If we _______ by train, we would avoid a traffic jam.
   A. go **B.** will go **C.** went
3. If you hadn't left early, you _______ heard his speech.
   A. had **B.** would **C.** would have
4. If you _______ me, I will be able to do it.
   A. help **B.** helped **C.** would help
5. If Tim really gets a tattoo, his father _______ very angry.
   A. is **B.** would be **C.** will be

7 **Look at Sally and describe her. Also, write what you think of her looks.**

For Whiz Kids

8 **Read the text about tattoos:**

Tattoos are becoming more and more popular today. Whereas in former times tattoos were associated with criminals or sailors they can nowadays be seen on celebrities and everyday people of all ages. Still people have mixed feelings when it comes to teenagers having them.
Adults often worry about the health risks associated with tattooing. Others see tattoos as a form of rebellion or immaturity. Another argument against teenagers getting inked is the fact that one's tastes change. What you like as a teenager might not be what you want to wear on your skin for the rest of your life. In many countries teenagers under a certain age therefore need their parents' consent if they want to have a tattoo.
But what is it that fascinates young people about tattoos? Some of them choose a design that has a deeper meaning for them and might remind them of a special person or event in their life. Some young people want to express their individuality or their beliefs.
If you want to have a tattoo, don't rush it. Think carefully before you make a decision. It might be a good idea to wait awhile before you have the tattoo done. If you still want it in a year, then get it. But don't forget to get your parents' consent if you are under 18. And be careful where you have it done. Only choose a professional tattoo artist who really knows what he/she is doing. Otherwise you risk damaging your health.

	true	false
1. Only prisoners and sailors have tattoos.	☐	☐
2. Adults often worry about teenagers having tattoos.	☐	☐
3. Every teenager can get a tattoo.	☐	☐
4. Many teenagers just choose any design.	☐	☐
5. It is better to think some time before you get a tattoo.	☐	☐
6. There are no health risks.	☐	☐
7. Fewer people have tattoos today than in former times.	☐	☐

Session 12 – Reading about superheroes

Do you remember?

Do the crossword puzzle!

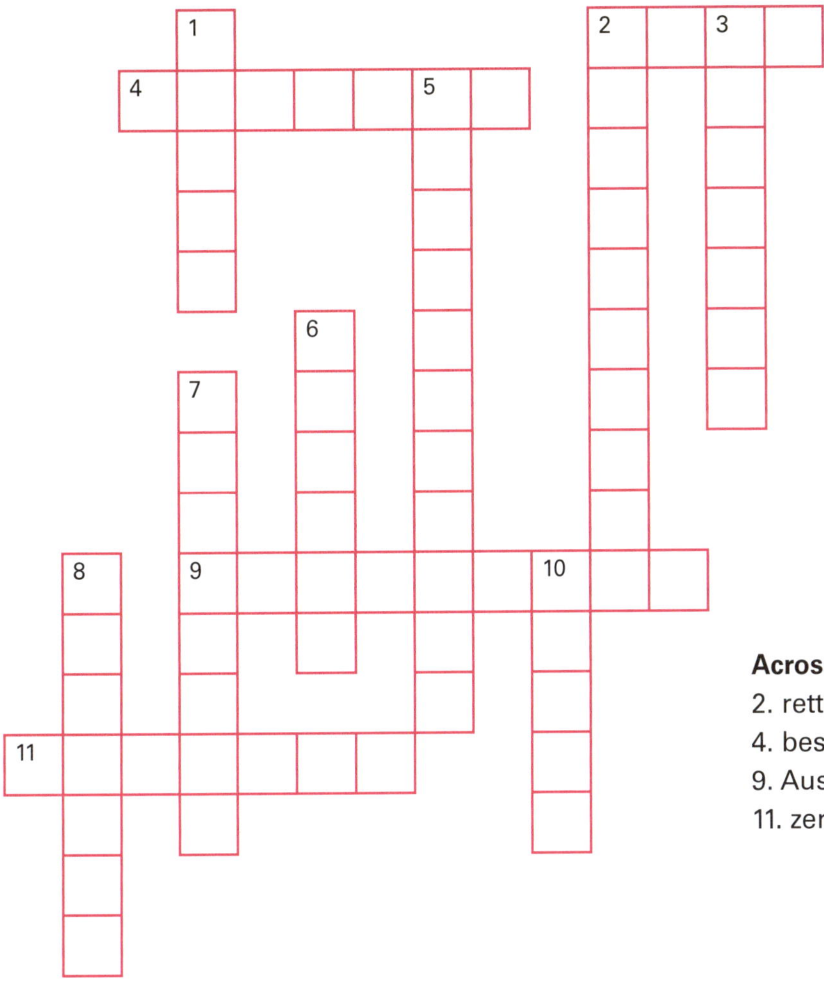

Across:
2. retten
4. beschützen
9. Ausrüstung
11. zerstören

Down:
1. tapfer
2. übermenschlich
3. Bösewicht
5. Katastrophe
6. Genie
7. Kraft
8. Freiheit
10. Feind

Practice

Complete the sentences using the –ing form of the verbs in the box:

ski	spend	build	smoke	move	see	draw	talk

1. I really enjoy ______ a quiet evening at home.
2. We are looking forward to ______ our friends again.
3. Stop ______ about Sam as if he were stupid.
4. It's a pity he is not good at ______.
5. Susan would really like to try ______ this winter.
6. I'm thinking of ______ to Vienna because all my friends live there.
7. Ask my sister, she is interested in ______ model planes.
8. I'm sorry but ______ is forbidden here.

3

5

Change the sentences so that they start with a gerund (–ing form):

1. You are forbidden to swim here.

____

2. It's interesting to read travel books.

____

3. It is difficult to solve crossword puzzles.

____

4. It is a hard job to save the world.

____

5. It is impossible for James to win this race.

____

4

Match the sentence halves:

1. I really like comics. I want to	☐ save the world.
2. Superheroes always try to	☐ help the people in the car.
3. Ironman tried to	☐ try drawing one myself.
4. We have decided to	☐ repair his suit of armour.
5. When he saw the accident he stopped to	☐ buy tickets for "The Avengers".

5

5

Fill in gerund or infinitive:

1. You must not forget __________ (water) the flowers.
2. It was such a nice evening. I really enjoyed __________ (talk) to your parents.
3. Would you please stop __________ (sing). I can't concentrate.
4. They decided __________ (stay) in the cheapest hotel in town.
5. My friends tried __________ (help) me with the work.

6

7

Put the questions and orders into reported speech:

1. Granddad said, "Don't talk to strange men!"

____

2. Sally asked, "Where did you get that cool shirt?"

____

3. The teacher asked, "Did you see the interesting documentary yesterday?"

____

4. Mother said to Paul, "Leave your sister alone!"

____

5. Peter asked his friend, "Have you talked to Mrs Miller about it?"

____

6. "Open the window, please", the lady said.

____

7. Tina asked, "When will I meet your girl-friend?"

____

For Whiz Kids

7 **Read the text about Spider Man and fill in the missing words from the box:**

developing	disappear	sixth sense	genetically	strength
	murdered	scientist	crush	

Peter Parker is a boy whose parents ______ after taking him to the home of his uncle Ben and his aunt May. Later Peter attends Midtown Science High School and has a ______ on Gwen Stacy.
When Peter finds some of his father's papers he learns that his dad worked at OsCorp with a ______ called Dr. Curt Connors. Peter wants to find out more and manages to get into OsCorp where he discovers a lab where ______ modified spiders are being created. He is bitten by one of these spiders.
After this bite he notices that he is ______ strange spider-like abilities. He can climb walls and ceilings, he has superhuman ______ and incredibly fast reflexes. He also develops a kind of ______ that warns him of dangers to come. He now calls himself Spider Man and after his uncle is ______ he begins to fight the evil that killed his uncle.

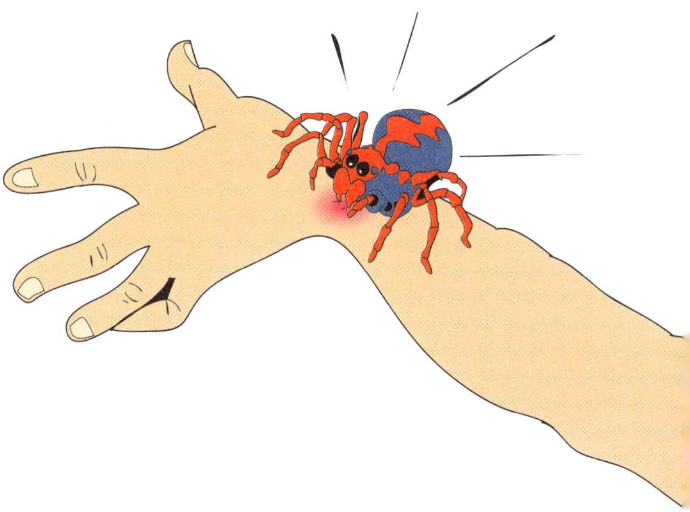

8 **What are Superheroes like? Find an adjective describing a superhero for each letter of the word.**

S ______________________________

U ______________________________

P ______________________________

E ______________________________

R ______________________________

H ______________________________

E ______________________________

R ______________________________

O ______________________________

PROGRESS CHECK

1 **Do the crossword. Find the English expressions:**

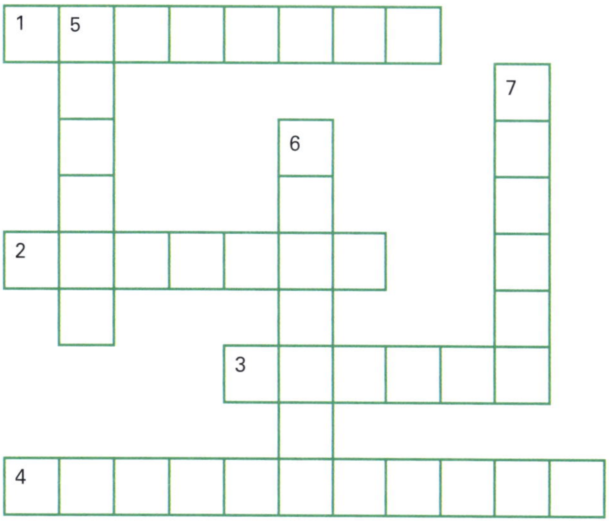

Across:
1. Beweis
2. Zeuge
3. Waffe
4. (polizeilich) untersuchen

Down:
5. Opfer
6. Verdächtige/r
7. Gefängnis

2 **Put the following sentences into reported speech:**

1. My friend Ruth wanted to know, "What did you like best about your trip to Ireland?"
   ____
2. Alex told us, "We didn't know that you are not allowed to go off-road on Aborigine land."
   ____
3. Mike asked, "Did you fly or drive to Alice Springs?"
   ____
4. His uncle warned him, "Don't walk around alone at night in a big city. It is dangerous."
   ____
5. Mira admitted, "When I was 15 I wanted to get a tattoo but my parents said 'no'."
   ____
6. Tom wanted to know, "How do you like the new film about Superman?"
   ____
7. My teacher told me, "It's not easy to find the right kind of job. Some jobs are badly paid."
   ____

3 **Complete the if-sentences:**

1. If I ______ (know) that it was going to rain I ______ ______ (take) my umbrella. But I didn't and got all wet.
2. Thank God we had some water. If we ______ (not/take) two bottles of water with us, we ______ (be) in big trouble when the car broke down in the middle of nowhere.
3. The weather forecast predicts (=vorhersagen) sunshine for tomorrow. If it ______ (be) really sunny tomorrow, I ______ (go) for a long walk with the dogs.

4. I got another bad mark in my English test! – Well, if you ________________ (pay) more attention in class and ________________ (study) more, you ________________ (get) better grades.

4 **Change the sentences from passive to active or from active to passive:**

1. The Aborigines were driven off their land by white settlers.

____

2. Because of the economic crisis many companies fire a number of workers.

____

3. Ireland is also called the Emerald Isle by some people.

____

4. The airport authorities cancelled the flight to Moscow.

____

5. In some parts of the world people eat insects.

____

6. Organic farmers don't use pesticides.

____

5 **Can you find the 13 words hidden in the grid?**
They are about big cities, jobs, food, hobbies, books, body art, Fairtrade and Superheroes.

E	Z	T	O	U	R	I	S	T	S	F	E
N	G	X	Y	F	G	R	U	I	K	D	M
V	N	J	R	O	T	C	E	L	L	O	C
I	I	Q	M	X	D	F	B	E	F	U	A
R	C	S	R	V	A	M	I	V	L	S	T
O	R	G	A	N	I	C	F	O	O	D	W
N	E	U	F	C	L	Y	C	N	G	F	O
M	I	T	R	A	F	F	I	C	X	W	M
E	P	O	U	S	K	V	M	R	T	Z	A
N	U	T	R	I	T	I	O	U	S	V	N
T	B	V	M	T	U	S	C	H	J	W	O
I	K	L	A	F	R	E	B	M	U	L	P

Weitere Bände in dieser Reihe:

ISBN 978-3-7074-1621-3

ISBN 978-3-7074-1617-6

Wenn du deine Englischkenntnisse vertiefen möchtest, arbeite auch mit diesen Büchern:

ISBN 978-3-7074-0761

ISBN 978-3-7074-1198-0

LÖSUNGEN
LOCKER Aufsteigen
Englisch 4

Session 1 – Ireland

1 **Can you find 15 words that have something to do with Ireland?**
Dublin, leprechaun, Cliffs of Moher, Belfast, rain, protestants, Irish, shamrock, catholics, Glendalough, Guinness, sheep, Kilkenny, potatoes, pub

2 **Fill in the correct tense (past simple, past progressive, past perfect):**
Last summer Paul and Samantha **wanted** to fly to Ireland with their parents. They **had already packed** their suitcases and **were waiting** for the taxi to take them to the airport. When the taxi **arrived,** their mother **looked** into her handbag to make sure the tickets **were** there. But she **could not** find them. So everybody **started** looking for the tickets in the whole house while the taxi driver **was waiting** in front of the house. Suddenly their father **remembered** that he **had put** the tickets into his suitcase. Quickly he **took** them out and they **got** into the taxi. They **arrived** at the airport just in time to catch their plane.

3 **Look at the picture and write down what the members of her family were doing when Mrs. Brown came home:**
1. When Mrs. Brown came home, her eldest daughter Sally **was listening to music.**
2. Tom **was doing his homework.**
3. The twins **were playing table tennis.**
4. Her husband **was sitting** on the sofa **watching** TV.
5. The baby **was crying.**

4 **Fill in the gaps using personal and possessive pronouns:**
1. Hello Mike, this is **my** brother Bill. I don't know if you have met **him.**
2. Hey girls, what do **you** think? Shall **we** buy tickets for the concert? **My** father could get **them.**
3. Peter always talks about **his** cat Susi. I'd really like to see **her/it.**
4. Paula and I are in the same class. Yesterday **our** teacher asked **us** to prepare a presentation together.

5 **Read the text about St. Patrick and mark the sentences *true* or *false*:**
1. false, 2. true, 3. false, 4. false, 5. true, 6. false, 7. false, 8. false, 9. true, 10. true

Session 2 – Investigating a crime

1 **Match the English and the German words:**
blackmail – erpressen, witness – Zeuge, crime scene – Tatort, murderer – Mörder, suspect – Verdächtige/r, weapon – Waffe, investigate – untersuchen, evidence – Beweis, victim – Opfer, question – verhören

2 **Unscramble the crime words:**
1. evidence, 2. burglar, 3. weapon, 4. crime scene,
5. thief, 6. murder, 7. investigate, 8. witness

3 **Fill in the correct passive forms:**
1. The old man **was killed** by the burglar.
2. This case **has been investigated** for two months.
3. The murderer **has not been caught** yet.
4. Last week the criminal **was arrested** by the police.
5. The manager **is being blackmailed** by a former employee.
6. The burglar **was sent** to prison for two months.
7. After the weapon **had been found** the police looked for fingerprints.
8. The suspect **is being questioned** by the police.
9. The thief **was sentenced** to 5 months in prison.

4 **Fill in the past perfect tense:**

1. After the police **had caught** the suspect, they started questioning him.
2. As soon as they **had identified** the victim, they contacted the victim's relatives.
3. After he **had shot** his wife, he called the police.
4. He **had just hacked** into the bank's computer when the Internet went down. Tough luck!
5. The old lady **had just withdrawn** some money from the cash machine when a mugger hit her on the head and stole the money.
6. After they **had found** the dead body, they phoned the police.

5 **Complete the following if-clauses:**

1. If you don't lock your bike, somebody **will steal** it.
2. If they **had** more money, they would buy a burglar alarm.
3. What **would you do** if somebody attacked you?
4. If I witnessed a crime, I **would call** the police.
5. If they had a suspect, they **would question** him/her.
6. If the fingerprints are on record, they **will be able to arrest** the thief.
7. What will you do if somebody **breaks** into your house?

6 **Fill in past or past perfect tense:**

1. She **was** on her way to the train station. Suddenly she decided to go back because she wasn't quite sure, if she **had locked** the front door.
2. The witness **gave** them a good description of the robbers.
3. He could not remember where he **had parked** his car.
4. Police cars were standing in front of the bank because some masked men **had tried** to rob the bank.
5. "**Did you watch** CSI New York last Monday?"- "No, I couldn't because I **had to** study for a test."

7 **Change the sentences from active to passive:**

1. The bank **was robbed** by three men.
2. The suspect **will be questioned** by the police.
3. Fiona **was attacked** by a tall man and her handbag **was taken.**
4. Mr. Winters **is being blackmailed** by an unknown person.
5. A crime thriller **will be shot** in our village (by a famous director).
6. A crime **is reported** by a witness.

8 **Find the famous detective!**

1. investigate, 2. shoot, 3. evidence, 4. arrest, 5. steal, 6. coffin, 7. detective, 8. blackmail, 9. thief, 10. weapon, 11. solve, 12. victim, 13. witness, 14. suspect

Session 3 – Getting around in a big city

1 **Unscramble the letters and write down the things you may find in a big city:**

1. train station, 2. underground, 3. theatre, 4. cinema, 5. airport

2 **Where are they?**

1. Bill is in **Paris**.
2. Sally **is in London.**
3. Ben and Mary **are in New York.**
4. Susan **is in Vienna.**
5. Paul **is in Rome.**

3 **Underline the correct word in these sentences:**

1. You should always wear a crash helmet when you <u>*ride*</u> a bike.
2. Pete <u>*goes*</u> to school by bus.
3. Trains to the airport <u>*run*</u> every hour.
4. Yesterday I <u>*missed*</u> the school bus.
5. He was late because of the traffic <u>*jam*</u>.

4 **Tell your friend what Mr. Anderson said about life in a big city:**

Mr. Anderson said that he **had been living** in a big city for many years.
He told us that first **he had enjoyed** the busy life there.
Then he explained that **he still liked** it but **had** other plans for the future.
He added that **next year he was going to move** to a small village in the country.
He promised that **he would tell** us what life **was** like there.

5 **Change each sentence to direct speech:**

1. She said, "Peter often **goes** skiing in winter."
2. Ann said, "They **left** on Monday."
3. The teacher said, "**I will** talk to **your** parents."
4. Tina said, "I **am** working."
5. Tom said, "**I have** just **talked** to Sam."

6 **Complete the sentences using *say* or *tell*:**

1. Ann **said** goodbye to me and left.
2. Simon, **tell** us about your holiday. Did you have a nice time?
3. Don't just stand there! **Say** something!
4. I wonder where Sue is. She **said** she would be here at 8 o'clock.
5. Jack **told** me that he was fed up with his job.
6. The doctor **said** that I should rest for at least a week.
7. Don't **tell** anybody what I **said**. It's a secret just between us.

7 **Put the sentences into indirect speech:**

1. Sally said that I had to lock the door when I left the flat.
2. Simon said that he had had to wait 20 minutes for the train.
3. Mary said that they would buy tickets for the concert in the afternoon.
4. Peter shouted that he had not broken her/his glasses.

8 **Where are the things?**

1. The keys are **on the magazine.**
2. The English book is **under the bed.**
3. The mobile phone is **between the books.**
4. The red jacket is **behind the desk.**
5. The tea cup is **in front of the computer.**
6. The concert tickets are **in the bag.**

9 **Underline the correct word:**

1. He always goes for a walk <u>*in*</u> the evening.
2. I'm not going <u>*to*</u> school today.
3. Did you see the new show <u>*on*</u> TV yesterday?
4. The teacher walked <u>*into*</u> the classroom and sat down.
5. You have to wait <u>*in front of*</u> the theatre.
6. The Browns want to buy a house <u>*in*</u> the country.

10 **Fill in the correct prepositions:**

In the morning many people use the underground to go to work. Most of them travel **between** 7 and 10 o'clock. Then there is always a queue **in front of** the ticket machines. The trains are very crowded, too. **After** 10 o'clock the situation gets better. Fewer people use the underground then.
Lots of people also go to work **by** car. Some of them live **in/at** places that have no good public transport, others don't want to fight **for** a seat on crowded trains.
I live **next to/near** an underground station, which is very practical and saves time in the morning.

Session 4 – Learning about jobs

1 **What are their jobs?**

1. Sandra explains mathematics to children. She is a **teacher.**
2. Mr. Smith helps people who have toothache. He is a **dentist.**
3. Tim makes bread and rolls. He is a **baker.**
4. Paul repairs cars. He is a **mechanic.**
5. Alice sells clothes to people in a big store. She is a **shop assistant.**
6. Mrs. Anderson works in a restaurant where she serves the food. She is a **waitress.**
7. Andrew catches criminals. He is a **policeman.**

2 **Complete the definitions:**

1. A vet **helps sick animals.**
2. A surgeon **operates on people.**
3. An architect **designs buildings.**
4. A secretary **answers the phone, writes e-mails and arranges meetings.**
5. An engineer **plans the building of houses, machines, roads etc.**

3 **Complete the sentences using the correct form of a word from the box:**
1. The man, who had been arrested, wanted to talk to his **lawyer.**
2. Many **soldiers** were killed during the war.
3. The **nurse** changed Mr. Brown's bandage.
4. Once a year the **gardener** cuts the trees.
5. Sheldon is a **scientist** and works at the university.
6. After 9/11 the **fire fighters** were celebrated as heroes.
7. The Guggenheim Museum was designed by a famous **architect.**

4 **Choose the best word for each space:**
My brother has got a new **job** in the best restaurant in town. He does not work in the kitchen because he is no **cook,** he is a **waiter.** He takes people's **orders** and brings them their food and drinks.
Two months ago he saw a/an **advertisement** in the newspaper which said that they were looking for someone with a lot of **experience.** He wrote an e-mail to the manager and was asked to come for a/an **interview.** The manager liked him and he was **offered** the job.

5 **At the job interview Paul was asked a lot of questions. Put them into reported speech:**
1. The manager asked Paul **where he had seen the advertisement.**
2. He wanted to know **if he had worked at a restaurant before.**
3. The manager asked him **why he wanted that job.**
4. He wanted to know **if he could work in a team.**
5. He asked Paul **when he would be able to start.**

6 **What did the people want to know? Complete the sentences using reported speech:**
Bruno wanted to know where his mobile phone was.
The teacher wanted to know what we/they were doing.
Sally wanted to know when he/she/I/we/they had arrived.
Molly wanted to know what I had done.
Father wanted to know when the tree would be cut.

7 **Fill in the missing words to make correct comparisons:**
1. It takes **longer** to become a doctor **than** to become a shop assistant.
2. I think that was the **worst** job interview I ever had.
3. Working in an office is not **as interesting as** working in a laboratory.
4. I did not get paid **as much** in my old job **as** in my new one.
5. Cars are **more expensive than** bicycles.
6. Being a fire fighter is **more dangerous than** being a teacher.
7. Last night's show was **funnier than** today's.

Session 5 – Eating the right kind of food

1 **Match the adjectives about food with the definitions:**
1d, 2e, 3b, 4c, 5f, 6a

2 **Do you know these food words:**
Salatgurke – cucumber, Zwiebel – onion, Nudeln – pasta, Bohnen/Fisolen – (green) beans, Birne – pear, Ananas – pineapple, Kirschen – cherries, Pilze – mushrooms, Spiegelei – fried egg, Fleisch – meat

3 **Complete the if-sentences (type 3):**
1. You would not have got sick, if you **had not eaten** so much ice cream.
2. If I had known that you are a vegetarian, I **would not have offered** you any meat.
3. If she had bought carrots, she **could have made** a tasty carrot soup.
4. If he **had used** more spices, the dish would have tasted better.
5. They would not have had to go to a fast food restaurant, if you **had cooked** dinner.
6. I **would not have ordered** the soup if I had known that it contained mushrooms.

4 **Fast food versus junk food. Read the text, then answer the questions:**
1. Junk food contains high levels of calories salt, sugar and fat. It is bad for our health.
2. Salads, an apple, a banana, milk, eggs.
3. It clogs our arteries and we put on weight.
4. It's food that can be made in a short time.

5 **Complete the if-sentences (all types):**
1. If you follow the recipe, the dish **will be** okay.
2. If I met Jamie Oliver, I **would ask** him for an autograph.
3. Don't eat meat, if you **feel** sorry for the animals.

4. If you don't want to put on weight, **don't eat** a lot of junk food!
5. If he had not been in a hurry, he **would have eaten** a proper breakfast.
6. If you listened to your doctor, you **would know** that too much junk food can clog your arteries.

6 Use the past or past perfect tense:

1. After he **had finished** the pizza, he felt a bit sick.
2. She **decided** to become a vegetarian after she had watched a film about how animals were killed.
3. When the waiter **came** to their table, they **asked** for the menu.
4. He asked his mum to prepare his favourite dish, because he **had not eaten** it in a long time.
5. When she went out for lunch, she **ordered** a salad.

7 Read the text, then do the true/false exercise:

1. false, 2. false, 3. true, 4. true, 5. false

8 –Ing form or infinitive?

1. Martin has bought a book on Organic Farming. He wants **to know** more about it.
2. She has tried **to give** up meat, but she says it is very difficult for her.
3. He insisted on **buying** Fairtrade products.
4. My dad dreams of **changing** his job. He'd like to be a chef.
5. She is a vegetarian. She does not miss **eating** meat.

Session 6 – Going to Australia

1 The Australia Quiz – do you know the correct answers?

1c, 2c, 3b, 4a, 5b, 6a

2 Do you know what is described here?

1. Great Barrier Reef, 2. wallaby, 3. Sydney Opera House, 4. didgeridoo, 5. Ayers Rock/Uluru, 6. outback

3 Complete the if-sentences:

1. If you **want** to spend some time in the Australian outback, make sure you take enough water with you.
2. If I had gone to Australia last year, I **would have visited** the Great Barrier Reef.
3. If they went to Sydney, they **could take** a picture of the famous Opera House.
4. If the weather is nice, Jeff and Jenny **will climb** to the top ofThe Harbour Bridge in Sydney.
5. If you are ill but live far away from a town, the flying doctors **will help** you.
6. If you **were** an Aborigine, Uluru would not just be a tourist attraction.
7. If they **had gone** to Darwin, they could have visited Kakadu National Park.

4 Fill in the correct tenses:

In August Mona and her family **flew** to Australia. It **took** them almost two days to get to Sydney, the first stop of their trip.They **stayed** at a nice hotel and **did** a lot of sightseeing. On their first day they **went** to The Harbour Bridge because from the top you **have** a wonderful view. Mona's mum **didn't climb** to the top because she **is** afraid of heights.They also **took** photos of Sydney's famous Opera House and the beautiful harbour.
From Sydney they **flew** to Alice Springs because they **wanted** to drive to Ayers Rock from there. At Ayers Rock Mona met a tourist who said," If I **had known** how dangerous it is to climb Uluru, I **would not have tried** it. I almost **broke** my leg."
From Alice spring Mona's family **flew** to Darwin because they **wanted** to explore Kakadu National Park. Mona's brother Simon **loved** the goannas and the cave paintings best.
On the flight back to Austria Mona's dad said, "Next time we **will go** to the Great Barrier Reef because it **is** the largest coral reef in the world."

5 Use reported speech:

1. Mona's friend Alice asked **what Mona had liked** best about Australia.
2. Mona's dad said **that they had to rent** a car if **they wanted** to go to Ayers Rock.
3. Simon wanted to know **when the Aborigines had arrived** in Australia.
4. Simon wanted to know how far away **Sydney was** from Perth.
5. Mona asked the guide **what Koala bears ate**.

6 Do the crossword:

Across: James Cook, prisoners, corals
Down: Aborigines, outback, reef

Session 7 – Talking about (unusual) hobbies

1 Fill in the chart:

TENSE	SENTENCE
Present tense simple	She collects soft toys.
Present tense progressive/continuous	He is reorganizing his stamp collection.
Past tense simple	They dressed up as historical figures.
Past tense progressive/continuous	She was building a fantastic sand castle.
Present perfect simple	He has copied about 50 paintings by famous artists.
Present perfect progressive/continuous	He has been carving wooden animals since he was seven.
Past perfect simple	They had given away their tea bag collection.
Future tense	We will take part in an extreme ironing competition.

2 Can you find the hobbies?

rock climbing
horse riding
sailing
fencing
reading
knitting

3 Read the three texts about unusual hobbies, then do the tasks:

a. Answer the following questions:
   1. Gerda has been collecting tea bags for seven years.
   2. It was invented by Phil Shaw in 1997.
   3. She creates shoes, clothes, jewelry and other things.
   4. Duct tape is stiff and it doesn't breathe well.

b. Tick *true* or *false*:
   1. false, 2. true, 3. false, 4. true, 5. true

4 Use the past or present perfect tense to complete the dialogues:

1. **A** When I was a child I **collected** buttons. I **loved** the different colours, shapes and sizes. **Have you ever collected** anything?
   B No, I haven't. I **have never felt** the need to collect anything.
2. **A** **Did you see** the extreme ironing competitions on TV last night?
   B No, I didn't. I **had to** write an essay for my English class.
3. **A** Two days ago I **watched** a documentary about unusual hobbies. They **interviewed** a person who collects airsick bags.
   B What a crazy idea!
4. **A** **Have you heard** about this exhibition on sand art?
   B Yes, I **have already seen** some posters. I think it is an unusual hobby.

5 Match the questions and answers:

1d, 2f, 3a, 4b, 5c, 6e

6 Read the short texts and ask questions:

1. When did she take up horse riding?
2. How often did she go riding as a child? How often does she go riding now?
3. Why can she only go riding at the weekend?
4. When did Simon start playing football?
5. At what age did he join a football club?
6. What does he want to become once he has finished school?

Session 8 – Finding out about Fairtrade

1 Do the crossword puzzle!

Across:	**Down:**
4. profit	1. development
7. export	2. justice
11. pesticide	3. farmer
12. beans	5. tea
	6. coffee
	8. project
	9. trade
	10. price

2 Read the text about Fairtrade and answer the questions:

1. Fairtrade products usually come from poorer or developing countries.
2. The rich countries and the multinational companies make the rules.
3. It is difficult because the prices change often and very quickly. They often don't know if they will be able to sell their crop in the following year again.
4. They don't just change their job because there are no other jobs where they live.
5. You can recognize Fairtrade products by the Fairtrade Mark.

3 Put into reported speech:

1. You asked him if he could do that for you.
2. They asked if I had been in London the week before.
3. He said he would have finished that paper by five o'clock.
4. She said that she was not hungry at the moment.
5. He told me to be quiet.
6. She asked me where I had been.
7. Tom told me not to leave the room.

4 Complete the sentences with the passive forms of the verbs:

1. Cocoa **is imported** into Austria.
2. In the future farmers in poorer countries **will be paid** a fair price for their crops.
3. Yesterday we **were taken** to the airport by our parents.
4. Fairtrade bananas **are sold** in many Austrian supermarkets.
5. I **have never been invited** to the queen's garden party.

5 Make passive sentences:

1. My bag was found by a little girl yesterday.
2. The baby will be baptized next month.
3. I have never before been asked to give an opening speech.
4. Marmalade is made from oranges.

6 Put into reported speech:

Mrs. Brown told the Inspector that something terrible had happened. She had lost her sweet little dog. She said that he had jumped out of her car in front of her house and now she couldn't find him.
The Inspector said that he had two questions. He wanted to know where she lived and when the dog had jumped out of the car.
Mrs. Brown answered that she lived in 10 Pembroke Road. It had been 5 in the afternoon when the dog had jumped out. She asked the Inspector to find Timmy or she would be very unhappy.
The Inspector told her not to worry. He promised they would try everything to find him again. He was sure he would come home as soon as he was hungry.
Mrs. Brown told the Inspector that the dog had run away the week before and had come home three days later. She had been really worried.
The Inspector asked if any of her neighbours had seen the dog since the day before.
Mrs. Brown said that she did not know. She would go home and ask them.
The Inspector asked her to call him if she found out anything.
Mrs. Brown said that she certainly would.

Session 9 – Reading good books

1 Find the following words in the grid. Then write down their German meaning.

narrator – Erzähler
novel – Roman
chapter – Kapitel
comic – Comicheft/Geschichte in Bildern
fantasy (book) – Fantasie(roman)
hero – Held
review – Buchbesprechung
summary – Zusammenfassung
blurb – Klappentext; kurze Inhaltsangabe
publish – veröffentlichen
plot – Handlung
poem – Gedicht

2 Fill in the correct linking words: but, when, because, and, so

1. Anna loved adventure books **but** she hated horror stories.
2. Bob read "The Hunger Games" **and** watched the movie.
3. Sometimes Molly starts crying **when** she reads a sad story.
4. Susan was too old for children's books, **so** she bought a young adult novel.
5. Adam does not have a lot of books **because** he hates reading.

3 Fill in the correct reflexive pronouns:

1. There was nobody to talk to, so the boy started talking to **himself.**
2. The lady said, "Harry, make **yourself** at home. I'll be right back."
3. When the giant looked at **himself** in the mirror for the first time, he was shocked.
4. Last week my mum had to work all day, so my brother and I had to look after **ourselves.**
5. "This is a nice sweater. Did you knit it **yourself**?" – "Yes, I made it **myself**. My grandma showed me how to do it."
6. They did not know where they were and they asked **themselves** if they would ever find out of that jungle again.

4 Use linking words (and, but, although, because, or, so, when, who, which…) to connect the sentences:

1. This looks like a good book **but** unfortunately it is a bit thick.
2. Can you recommend a good book **because** I need to write a book report.
3. I didn't like "Nightmare" **although I** usually like horror books.
4. Jenny **who** is the main character of the book has a terrible secret.
5. Melanie wanted to read a good English book, **so** she asked her teacher for advice.
6. I have to write a summary of the first chapter **and** I also have to describe the main character.

5 Use the word given in capitals at the end of each line to form a word that fits in the gap in the same line:

I was walking down the street when a young man suddenly
appeared in front of me. "Please, help me!" he said. I could see from
his **expression** that he was really scared. He
spoke English with a Polish accent. He gave me a
flash drive and said, "There is top secret **information**
on this memory stick." Then he put a piece of paper with a name
and an address into my hand. "Contact this person, but do it
secretly. If anybody finds out you have this
flash drive, your life will be in danger." I didn't really understand
what was going on but when I looked up, the young man was
gone.

7 What are the American expressions for the following words?

flat	**apartment**	crisps	**chips**
ground floor	**first floor**	underground	**subway**
post	**mail**	chips	**French fries**
pavement	**sidewalk**	film	**movie**
lift	**elevator**	holidays	**vacation**

Session 10 – Exploring space

1 Can you find the 12 "space" words in the grid?
spaceshuttle, alien, orbit, earth, universe, astronaut, spaceship, robots, explore, UFO, planet, rocket

3 Complete the sentences with the –ing form of the verbs from the box:
1. I enjoy **watching** documentaries about space travel.
2. Ken is interested in **reading** about aliens and life in outer space.
3. My sister is thinking about **applying** for a job with NASA.
4. He is looking forward to **meeting** a real astronaut for the first time.
5. I'm sure that **travelling** into space will be possible in the future.
6. My dad remembers **seeing** the space shuttle disaster of 2003 on TV.
7. Stop **laughing** and finish the text about Neil Armstrong, the first man on the Moon.

4 If the verb in bold (fettgedruckt) is correct, put a tick into the box.
If it is wrong, write down the correct form of the verb.
1. I hope I'll be able **to travel** into space when I am older.
2. My mum suggested **watching** a science fiction movie but I hate science fiction.
3. I'd really like **to visit** the Kennedy Space Center one day. I have heard so much about it.
4. Stop **talking** and start reading the text about astronauts.
5. Where is my fantasy book? I remember **putting** it on my desk.
6. I can't imagine **having** to live without a computer or a TV set.
7. The children enjoyed **reading** about aliens and robots.
8. On the way to the Science Museum we stopped **to have** lunch at a fast food restaurant.

5 Fill in the correct prepositions:
1. Neil Armstrong was the first man to set foot **on** the Moon.
2. The Moon landing was watched **by** half a million people.
3. There are a number of people who would like to travel **into** space.
4. A number of books have been written **about** the Apollo missions.
5. The *Columbia* broke **up** when it re-entered the earth's atmosphere.
6. **In** 1986 the *Challenger* exploded shortly after take-off.
7. The taste **of** food often changes in space.

6 Read the two short texts, then do the *true/false* exercise:
1. true, 2. false, 3. false, 4. true, 5. true, 6. false

7 Find the mistakes (there is one in each sentence) and write down the correct sentences:
1. In the movie MiB agents Kay and Jay **were attacked** by violent aliens.
2. The aliens in Independence Day wanted **to take** over the world.
3. The Science Museum **is closed** on Christmas Day.
4. The kids are **looking** forward to visiting the Space Center.
5. All of a sudden one of the engines stopped **working** but the astronauts did not panic.

Session 11 – Looking at body art

1 Can you remember the parts of the body?
wrist, knee, elbow, finger, mouth, head, lips, tongue, shoulder, stomach

2 Complete the sentences using the correct form of a word from the box:
1. **May** I take a look at your new tattoo?
2. Sorry, but you **must not** smoke in here.
3. You **should** think again before having your lip pierced.
4. **Could** you pass the salt, please?
5. Excuse me, **may** I ask you something?
6. I'm not sure where John is. He **might** be in the cellar.

3 Rewrite the sentences using *might, must* or *can't*:
1. This dragon tattoo must be new.
2. I might have my nose pierced.
3. That can't be the right way.
4. You might be sorry if you shave your head.
5. This must be her brother.

4 Complete the sentences using one word for each space:

1. Peter was not at the party yesterday. He **had** to work.
2. Someone **must** be at home. The lights are on.
3. You **should** really work harder, then your marks will be better.
4. I can't find my keys. Well, I **might/must** have left them in the car.
5. Do you really **have** to leave now?
6. The baby has been crying for an hour. She **must** be tired soon.
7. You **can't** be serious! I'd never do that.
8. **May** I leave the table now?

5 Complete the if-sentences:

Your sentences could look like this:

1. If you really want a pierced nose, **you will have to look for a good piercing studio.**
2. I would have dyed my hair purple **if my parents had not been against it.**
3. If we hadn't been late, **we would have met Peter.**
4. If the boys were at home, **we would hear them.**
5. If you really get a tattoo, **your mother will be so angry.**
6. If getting pierced did not hurt, **more people would be pierced.**
7. If I had known how painful getting a tattoo is, **I would not have one.**

6 Choose the most suitable word or phrase:

1. If you start now, you **won't** be late for the meeting.
2. If we **went** by train, we would avoid a traffic jam.
3. If you hadn't left early, you **would have** heard his speech.
4. If you **help** me, I will be able to do it.
5. If Tim really gets a tattoo, his father **will be** very angry.

8 Read the text about tattoos:

1. false, 2. true, 3. false, 4. false, 5. true, 6. false, 7. false

Session 12 – Reading about superheroes

1 Do the crossword puzzle!

Across:	**Down:**
2. save	1. brave
4. protect	2. superhuman
9. equipment	3. villain
11. destroy	5. catastrophy
	6. genius
	7. strength
	8. freedom
	10. enemy

2 Complete the sentences using the –ing form of the verbs in the box:

1. I really enjoy **spending** a quiet evening at home.
2. We are looking forward to **seeing** our friends again.
3. Stop **talking** about Sam as if he were stupid.
4. It's a pity he is not good at **drawing**.
5. Susan would really like to try **skiing** this winter.
6. I'm thinking of **moving** to Vienna because all my friends live there.
7. Ask my sister, she is interested in **building** model planes.
8. I'm sorry but **smoking** is forbidden here.

3 Change the sentences so that they start with a gerund (–ing form):

1. Swimming is forbidden here.
2. Reading travel books is interesting.
3. Solving crossword puzzles is difficult.
4. Saving the world is a hard job.
5. Winning the race is impossible for James.

4 Match the sentence halves:

1. I really like comics. I want to try drawing one myself.
2. Superheroes always try to save the world.
3. Ironman tried to repair his suit of armour.
4. We have decided to buy tickets for "The Avengers".
5. When he saw the accident he stopped to help the people in the car.

5 Fill in gerund or infinitive:

1. You must not forget **to water** the flowers.
2. It was such a nice evening. I really enjoyed **talking** to your parents.
3. Would you please stop **singing.** I can't concentrate.
4. They decided **to stay** in the cheapest hotel in town.
5. My friends tried **to help** me with the work.

6 Put the questions and orders into reported speech:

1. Granddad told me not to talk to strange men.
2. Sally asked where I had got that cool shirt.
3. The teacher asked us if we had seen the interesting documentary the day before.
4. Mother told Paul to leave his sister alone.
5. Peter asked his friend if she had talked to Mrs Miller about it.
6. The lady asked me to open the window.
7. Tina asked when she would meet his girl-friend.

7 Read the text about Spider Man and fill in the missing words from the box:

Peter Parker is a boy whose parents **disappear** after taking him to the home of his uncle Ben and his aunt May. Later Peter attends Midtown Science High School and has a **crush** on Gwen Stacy.

When Peter finds some of his father's papers he learns that his dad worked at OsCorp with a **scientist** called Dr. Curt Connors. Peter wants to find out more and manages to get into OsCorp where he discovers a lab where **genetically** modified spiders are being created. He is bitten by one of these spiders.

After this bite he notices that he is **developing** strange spider-like abilities. He can climb walls and ceilings, he has superhuman **strength** and incredibly fast reflexes. He also develops a kind of **sixth sense** that warns him of dangers to come. He now calls himself Spider Man and after his uncle is **murdered** he begins to fight the evil that killed his uncle.

Progress Check

1 Do the crossword. Find the English expressions:

Across:
1. evidence
2. witness
3. weapon
4. investigate

Down:
5. victim
6. suspect
7. prison

2 Put the following sentences into reported speech:

1. My friend Ruth wanted to know what I/we had liked best about my/our trip to Ireland.
2. Alex told us that they hadn't known that you were not allowed to go off-road on Aborigine land.
3. Mike asked if I/we/they/he/she had driven or flown to Alice Springs.
4. His uncle warned him not to walk around alone at night in a big city. It was dangerous.
5. Mira admitted that when she had been 15 she had wanted to get a tattoo but her parents had said 'no'.
6 Tom wanted to know how I /we/they/she/he liked the new film about Superman.
7. My teacher told me that it was not easy to find the right kind of job. Some jobs were badly paid.

3 Complete the if-sentences:

1. If I **had known** that it was going to rain I **would have taken** my umbrella. But I didn't and got all wet.
2. Thank God we had some water. If we **had not taken** two bottles of water with us, we **would have been** in big trouble when the car broke down in the middle of nowhere.
3. The weather forecast predicts (=vorhersagen) sunshine for tomorrow. If it **is** really sunny tomorrow, I **will go** for a long walk with the dogs.
4. I got another bad mark in my English test! – Well, if you **paid** more attention in class and **studied** more, you **would get** better grades.

4 Change the sentences from passive to active or from active to passive:

1. White settlers drove the Aborigines off their land.
2. A number of workers are fired because of the economic crisis (by many companies).
3. Some people also call Ireland the Emerald Isle.
4. The flight to Moscow was cancelled by the airport authorities.
5. In some parts of the world insects are eaten (by people).
6. Pesticides are not used by organic farmers.

5 **Can you find the 13 words hidden in the grid? They are about big cities, jobs, food, hobbies, books, body art, Fairtrade and Superheroes.**

tourists, collector, organic food, traffic, nutritious, plumber, environment, piercing, farm, comic, novel, golf, catwoman